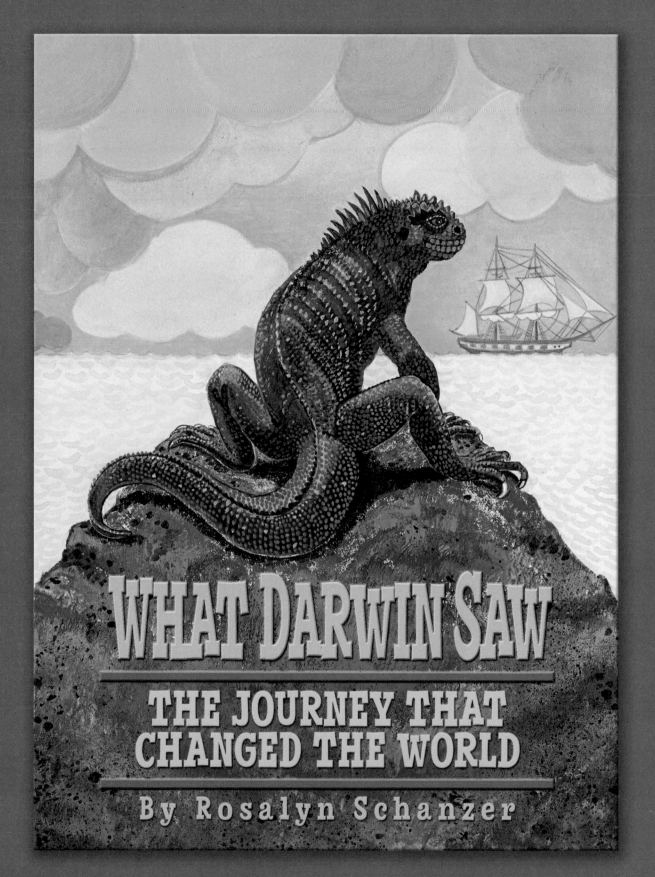

WHAT DARWIN SAW

THE JOURNEY THAT CHANGED THE WORLD

By Rosalyn Schanzer

NATIONAL GEOGRAPHIC

WASHINGTON, D.C.

THIS BOOK IS DEDICATED TO MY GRANDFATHER, THE LATE RABBI JEROME MARK

During the Scopes Monkey Trial of 1925 in Dayton, Tennessee, he worked with defense lawyer Clarence Darrow as an expert consultant on the Old Testament of the Bible. He helped Darrow think of questions that would trap prosecution lawyer William Jennings Bryan into admitting that the Bible could not always be interpreted literally and that every living thing on Earth could not have been created in six days a few thousand years ago. Darrow's interrogation of Bryan was front-page news all over America and helped gain widespread support for Charles Darwin's famous Theory of Evolution. R.S.

This story features abridged quotes gleaned from Charles Darwin's *Beagle* diary, his letters, and his books and scientific papers. Darwin's quotes are set in brown type. The author's text is set in black type. Quotes from everyone else are set in orange type.

The author has updated Darwin's spelling and punctuation slightly to make reading easier for young people.

Library of Congress Cataloging-in-Publication Data

Schanzer, Rosalyn.
  What Darwin saw : the journey that changed the world / by Rosalyn Schanzer.
    p. cm.
  ISBN 978-1-4263-0396-8 (hardcover : alk. paper)—ISBN 978-1-4263-0397-5 (library binding : alk. paper)
  1. Darwin, Charles, 1809-1882—Juvenile literature. 2. Darwin, Charles, 1809-1882—Travel—Juvenile literature. 3. Beagle Expedition (1831-1836)—Juvenile literature. 4. Naturalists—England—Biography—Juvenile literature. I. Title.
  QH31.D2S28 2009
    508.092—dc22

                    2008039809

Founded in 1888, the National Geographic Society is one of the largest nonprofit scientific and educational organizations in the world. It reaches more than 285 million people worldwide each month through its official journal, NATIONAL GEOGRAPHIC, and its four other magazines; the National Geographic Channel; television documentaries; radio programs; films; books; videos and DVDs; maps; and interactive media. National Geographic has funded more than 8,000 scientific research projects and supports an education program combating geographic illiteracy.

For more information, please call 1-800-NGS LINE (647-5463) or write to the following address:

NATIONAL GEOGRAPHIC SOCIETY
1145 17th Street N.W.
Washington, D.C. 20036-4688 U.S.A.

Visit the Society's Web site: www.nationalgeographic.com/books
For librarians and teachers: www.ngchildrensbooks.com
For more for kids from National Geographic: kids.nationalgeographic.com

For information about special discounts for bulk purchases, please contact National Geographic Books Special Sales: ngspecsales@ngs.org

For rights or permissions inquiries, please contact National Geographic Books Subsidiary rights: ngbookrights@ngs.org

You can reach the author at www.rosalynschanzer.com

Printed in the U.S.A.

London, England

CHARLES DARWIN

Born February 12, 1809
(the same day as Abraham Lincoln)

This is Charles Darwin, a popular 22-year-old who loves to hunt, ride fast horses, and collect all sorts of things from rocks to small sea creatures to beetles. Even though Darwin has never been much of a student, he is destined to become one of the greatest scientists in history. And why is that? It is because Darwin's astonishing discoveries will forever change the way people think about our planet and every single thing that lives here.

Darwin has just been offered the post of naturalist-companion to the captain of Her Majesty's Ship *Beagle*. This well-built little sailing vessel has been specially fitted out to make a scientific voyage all the way around the world. Carrying an excellent crew of 74 men, it's under orders to chart the coast of South America and to figure out the correct longitude of certain places in the South Pacific. Darwin's great adventure will last four years, ten months, and two days. It will affect everything he does for the rest of his life.

How can that be? To find out, let's join young Charles Darwin himself as he tells the story in his own words. You can even follow his journey by looking at the map on pages 46 and 47.

ROBERT FITZROY
Captain of the Beagle

CHARLES DARWIN

The Voyage Begins

DECEMBER 27, 1831

Bag of Tricks

I proved today the utility of a contrivance which will afford me hours of amusement — it is a bag four feet deep, made of bunting, & dragged behind the vessel. This evening it brought up a mass of small animals.

This sea-slug, when disturbed, emits a fine purplish-red fluid. Besides this means of defense, an acrid secretion spread over its body causes a sharp, stinging sensation.

The cuttle-fish escape detection by a chameleon-like power of changing color. While looking for marine animals, I was saluted by a jet of water accompanied by a grating noise. Afterwards I found out that it was the cuttle-fish concealed in a hole.

One day I was amused by watching the habits of the Diodon antennatus, which was caught swimming near the shore. This fish, with its flabby skin, is known to possess the singular power of distending itself into a nearly spherical form.

In the forenoon a water-spout took place. When they approach a vessel, it is usual to fire a big gun in order to break them.

Notes from a Brazilian Forest

April 4, 1832—The *Beagle* sails alongside porpoises, sharks, turtles, and great numbers of ships. The little vessel passes beneath world-famous Sugarloaf Mountain and other wild and stony peaks, and in most glorious style, it enters the harbor at Rio de Janeiro, Brazil.

Darwin and five other men promptly set out by horseback and canoe on an excursion through Brazil's exotic interior. Never has he imagined such an enormous variety of plants and animals.

Too Many Animals to Count

In a single day, Darwin collects 68 different types of a tiny beetle! He discovers more strange animals, too.

On the road we saw many beautiful toucans. Amused by watching humming birds.

A small frog sits on a blade of grass and sends forth a pleasing chirp: when several are together they sing in harmony.

This is the only butterfly I have ever seen that uses its legs for running.

EEEK!

Astonished at the labors of ants burdened with pieces of green leaf larger than their own bodies.

Eat or Be Eaten

Though turquoise oceans and forests filled with orchids may be beautiful, danger lurks at every turn. Both are worlds of predators—and of prey.

Monkeys can escape capture by swinging through the trees with their tails.

Bearded monkeys have prehensile tails which even after death can support the whole weight of the body.

This phasmid stick can stand right in front of its enemies without getting eaten because it looks exactly like a twig.

An onrushing army of tiny black ants darkens every stalk and leaf in its path, surrounding and killing a fleeing horde of spiders, cockroaches, and other insects, and even a few lizards.

Human Beings Can Be Predators & Prey, Too

How weak are the arguments of those who maintain that slavery is a tolerable evil! The Corcovado is notorious for run-away slaves. We met three villainous looking ruffians armed up to the teeth. They were slave-hunters, & receive so much for every man dead or alive whom they may take.

Hungry enemies of the snipe might never even see it because the colors of its feathers make such great camouflage.

Many predators are fantastic fighters equipped with horns, claws, poisons, or sharp teeth. One day, Darwin sees a ferocious battle between a huge spider and a Pepsis wasp (the wasp wins with its vicious sting).

The vampire bat is often the cause of much trouble, by biting the horses on their withers.

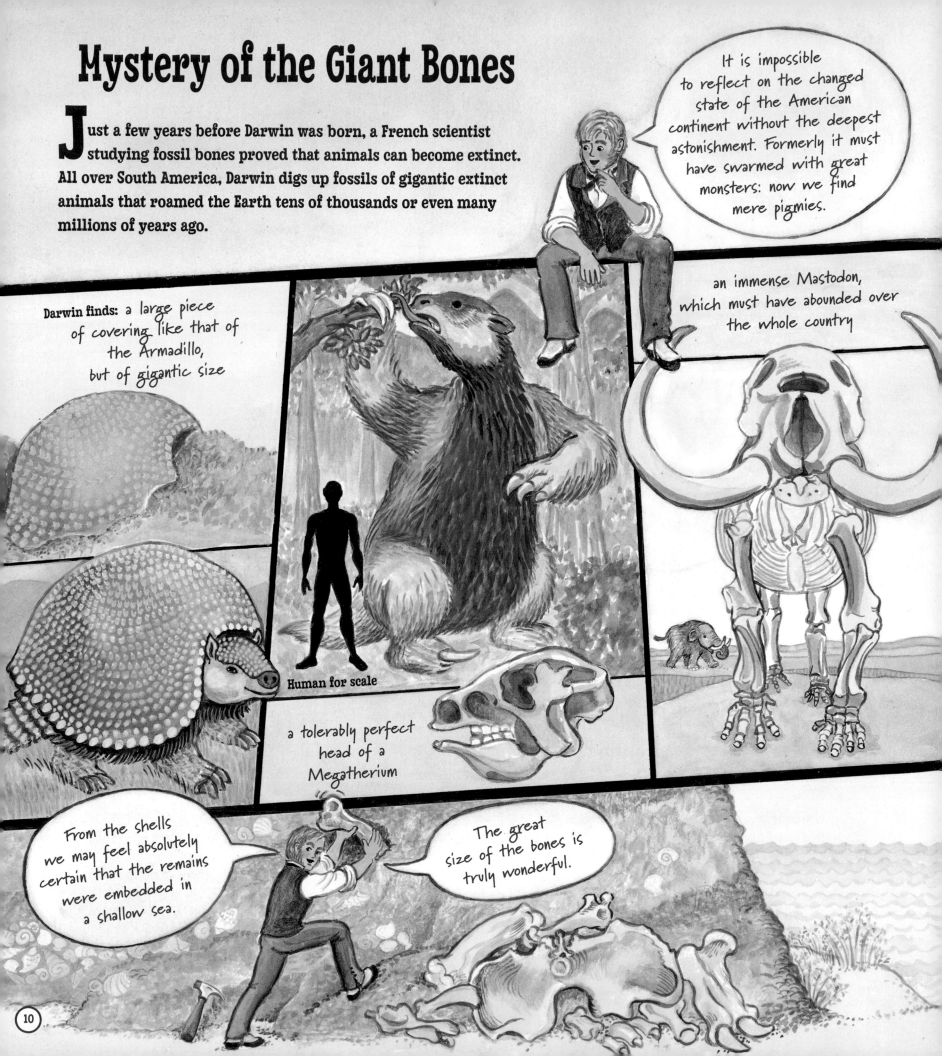

Mystery of the Giant Bones

Just a few years before Darwin was born, a French scientist studying fossil bones proved that animals can become extinct. All over South America, Darwin digs up fossils of gigantic extinct animals that roamed the Earth tens of thousands or even many millions of years ago.

It is impossible to reflect on the changed state of the American continent without the deepest astonishment. Formerly it must have swarmed with great monsters: now we find mere pigmies.

Darwin finds: a large piece of covering like that of the Armadillo, but of gigantic size

an immense Mastodon, which must have abounded over the whole country

Human for scale

a tolerably perfect head of a Megatherium

From the shells we may feel absolutely certain that the remains were embedded in a shallow sea.

The great size of the bones is truly wonderful.

10

The country is a broken mass of wild rocks, lofty hills & useless forests, & these are viewed through mists & endless storms.

The *Beagle* braves a month of gigantic waves, and it almost crashes as the crew struggles to survey the coast of Tierra del Fuego.

Tierra del Fuego: A Tale of Change and Survival

The captain has his own reasons for coming here. Darwin explains:

During [a] former voyage, Captain FitzRoy seized a party of natives, and some of these he took with him to England to educate at his own expense. To settle these natives in their own country was one chief inducement to Captain FitzRoy to undertake our present voyage.

I was struck, whilst living with the Fuegians on board the Beagle, [by] how similar their minds were to ours.

A universal favorite. Merry and often laughed. Fond of admiring himself in a looking glass.

Jemmy Button

York Minster

A full-grown short powerful man. Reserved, morose; his intellect good.

Fuegia Basket

A nice modest young girl, very quick in learning languages. York Minster determined to marry her as soon as they were on shore.

When the *Beagle* sets anchor, its crew is surrounded by Fuegians.

Captain FitzRoy is sure his three students are happy to be "civilized" and will gladly teach their tribesmen a modern way of life. He is devastated when the Fuegians almost immediately return to their own cultural roots and have no intention of living the English way.

And so Darwin asks himself a few questions.

Perhaps [nothing] is more sure to create astonishment than the first sight, in his native haunt, of a real barbarian. I believe, in this extreme part of South America, man exists in a lower state of improvement than in any other part of the world. At night, human beings, naked and scarcely protected from the wind and rain, sleep on the wet ground coiled up like animals.

[Yet] nature has fitted the Fuegian to the climate & productions of his country.

Whence have these people come? Have they remained in the same state since the creation of the world? Could our [ancestors] have been men like these?

Darwin waves goodbye to Jemmy Button.

Riding with Gauchos

While FitzRoy is surveying the coast of South America, Darwin explores the vast inland plain called the pampas. He travels on horseback with bands of tough cowboys called gauchos and joyously learns how they live off the land.

The wild Gaucho cavalry formed the most savage picturesque group I ever beheld. They are singularly striking; great spurs clanking on their heels & a knife, stuck (& often used) as a dagger at their waist. Gauchos sleep on the bare ground at all times & as they travel get their food.

I saw one most beautiful chase; a fine Ostrich tried to escape; the Gauchos pursued it at a reckless pace, each man whirling the balls round his head; the foremost at last threw them: in an instant the Ostrich rolled over & over, its legs being lashed together by the thong.

A tiny desert toad "drinks" dew through its skin.

Flamingos drink from a salty lake.

Condor

Puma

Guanaco

A capybara (water-hog) swims with its babies.

A scissor-beak catches a fish.

14

An armadillo eats a snake.

Rheas run but can't fly; the male alone hatches the eggs.

A frightened lizard plays dead.

The zorillo fears neither dog nor man.

15

Battle Cry

Darwin sees firsthand how Europeans are competing for land in South America. And they are winning. In Patagonia, Spanish cattle barons intend to claim all the Indians' territory and turn it into grazing land. Due to the weapons and superior numbers of Argentina's brutal army, Darwin fears that the Indians who have lived on these lands since time immemorial will be wiped out.

AUGUST 1833

Some months ago the government of Buenos Ayres sent out an army to exterminate the Indians. I believe such a villainous Banditti-like army was never before collected together.

Soon entire tribes of plains Indians are fleeing farther and farther toward the Andes Mountains. They are running for their lives.

Two hundred soldiers first discovered Indians by a cloud of dust from their horses. The country was mountainous and wild. The Indians, men, women, and children, were about one hundred and ten in number, and they were nearly all taken or killed, for the soldiers sabre every man. The Indians are now so terrified that each flies; but when overtaken, like wild animals, they fight against any number to the last moment.

Who would believe in this civilized country that such atrocities were committed? The children of the Indians are sold or given away as slaves.

Human beings are not the only colonizers of the New World.

European cardoon occurs across the continent. I saw several hundred square miles covered by one mass of these prickly plants, impenetrable by man or beast. Where these great beds occur, nothing else can now live.

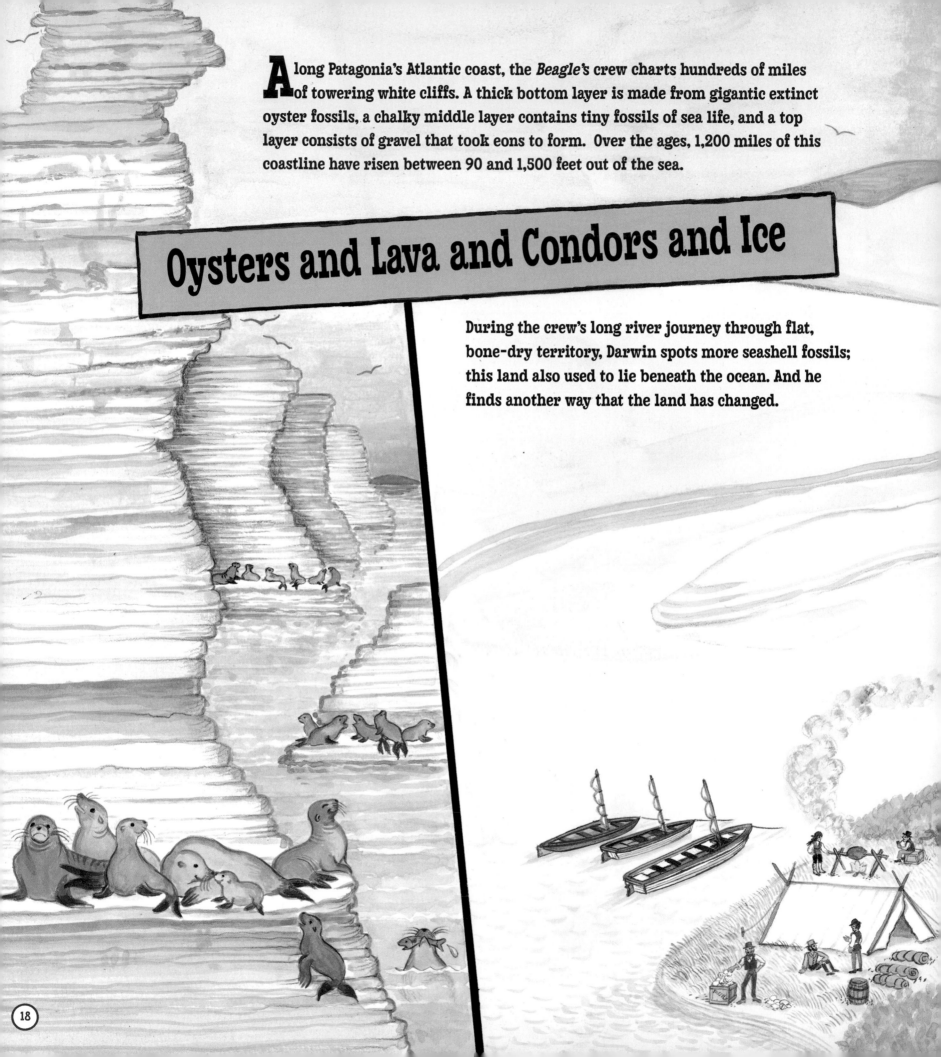

Along Patagonia's Atlantic coast, the *Beagle*'s crew charts hundreds of miles of towering white cliffs. A thick bottom layer is made from gigantic extinct oyster fossils, a chalky middle layer contains tiny fossils of sea life, and a top layer consists of gravel that took eons to form. Over the ages, 1,200 miles of this coastline have risen between 90 and 1,500 feet out of the sea.

Oysters and Lava and Condors and Ice

During the crew's long river journey through flat, bone-dry territory, Darwin spots more seashell fossils; this land also used to lie beneath the ocean. And he finds another way that the land has changed.

The plains are capped by a field of Lava, which at some remote period poured forth from the Andes. Lava further up the river is more than 300 feet thick.

The Lava caused many small springs. It is curious how the scenery is dependent on geology. The river is narrower, hence the stream more rapid; in the channel there are great blocks of Lava.

Wherever such changes occurred, plants and animals changed too. As the land rose from the sea, the giant oysters disappeared and were replaced by far smaller oysters in different waters. When lava formed cliffs above the dried-out seabed, new kinds of wildlife found a home.

Condors are magnificent birds never found excepting where there are perpendicular cliffs; it was a fine sight to see between ten & twenty Condors wheel away in majestic circles.

As the *Beagle* sails around the bottom tip of South America and into the Pacific Ocean, Darwin watches two other forces reshape the earth.

Every valley is filled with a glacier leading its blue stream of ice to a bold precipice overhanging the sea. Great masses of ice fall from these cliffs, and the crash reverberates like the broadside of a man-of-war.

There are numberless rocks on which the Pacific incessantly rages. We passed between the East & West Furies, and there are so many breakers that the sea is called the Milky Way.

Volcanoes

JANUARY 19, 1835
ISLA GRANDE DE CHILO

Suddenly there are signs that the earth is about to change right now—and fast!

During this night the Volcano of Osorno was in great activity. At midnight the sentry observed something like a large star, which increased in size till it presented a magnificent spectacle; Large masses of molten matter were projected upwards and burst in the air, assuming many fantastical forms.

I was surprised at hearing afterwards that Aconcagua in Chile, 480 miles northwards, was in action on this same night; and still more surprised to hear that the great eruption of Coseguina (2,700 miles north of Aconcagua), accompanied by an earthquake felt over 1,000 miles, occurred within six hours of this same time.

23

The series of volcanic eruptions has signaled an even greater upheaval. On February 20, 1835, two thundering explosions of smoke and foam shoot forth from the ocean. In an instant, the water turns black. It smells horrible, and the sea appears to be boiling. At the same time in an area hundreds of miles long, the very crust of the earth bursts violently apart.

. . . and

Terrible news! Not a house in Concepcion or Talcahuano was standing. Seventy villages were destroyed, & a great wave almost washed away the ruins of Talcahuano.

People running outside scarcely passed their thresholds before the houses fell in. In a large boarding school, the beds were buried 8 feet beneath bricks, yet all the young ladies escaped.

Hundreds had no means of procuring food. Thieves prowled about; with one hand they beat their breasts and with the other filched from the ruins.

Earthquakes!

Cows standing on the steep side of the island of Quiriquina were rolled into the sea. Dogs generally during an Earthquake howl, but this time they all quietly left the town minutes before the shock. On the same morning wonderfully large flocks of sea birds were directing their course inland.

A little English boy 4 or 5 years old & an old woman got into a boat, but it was cut into two; the old woman was drowned but the little boy was carried out to sea, & was picked up some hours afterwards quietly seated on the thwart.

The most remarkable effect of this earthquake was the permanent elevation of the land. Captain FitzRoy found putrid mussel shells adhering to the rocks ten feet above the High-water mark; the inhabitants had formerly dived for these shells. Nothing is so unstable as the level of the earth.

Children making boats with old tables & chairs appear as happy as their parents are miserable.

Galápagos: A Different Set of Beings

On September 7, 1835, the ship sets sail for the Galápagos Archipelago, a group of ten newly formed volcanic islands straddling the Equator about 600 miles west of South America. Eight days later, the voyagers arrive at one of the strangest places on Earth.

CHATHAM ISLAND

The whole is black lava thrown into rugged waves, crossed by great fissures, and covered by intricate thickets. The day was glowing hot. As I was scrambling over the rough surface, I met two large tortoises, each of which must have weighed two hundred pounds. One gave a deep loud hiss and drew in its head. They seemed like animals from some other planet.

The inhabitants can distinguish the tortoises from the different islands. Besides three kinds of Turtles, the Tortoise is so abundant that a single Ship's company here caught from 500-800 in a short time. The breast-plate with the meat attached to it is roasted as the Gauchos do. It is very good, and the young tortoises make an excellent soup. Mr Lawson recollects having seen a Terrapin which 6 men could scarcely lift & two could not turn over on its back.

At Charles Island, I saw a boy by the side of a well with a long stick in his hand. As the doves came to drink he killed as many as he wanted & in half an hour collected them together & carried them to the house for dinner.

The birds are Strangers to Man & think him as innocent as their countrymen the huge Tortoises. Mr. King killed one with his hat & I pushed a large Hawk off a branch with the end of my gun. One day, a mocking-bird alighted on the edge of a pitcher made of the shell of a tortoise, which I held in my hand whilst lying down. It began very quietly to sip the water, and allowed me to lift it with the vessel from the ground.

Albemarle Island is composed of 6 or 7 great Volcanic Mounds covered with immense streams of black naked lava which, having flowed over the rims of the great caldrons, spread over miles of the sea-coast.

The rocks on the coast abounded with great black lizards, and on the hills, a yellowish orange species was equally common. They are considered good food; this day forty were collected.

The large yellow Lizard's burrows are so numerous that we had difficulty finding a spot to pitch the tents. Never drinking water, they like succulent Cactus, & will, like dogs, struggle [and] seize it from another.

JAMES ISLAND

The tortoise is very fond of water and wallowing in mud. Well-beaten paths radiate off in every direction from wells at a considerable elevation down to the sea-coast. Near the springs it was comical to behold many of these great monsters; one set eagerly traveling onwards with outstretched necks, and another set returning, after having drunk their fill. When the tortoise arrives at the spring, it buries its head in the water above its eyes, and greedily swallows great mouthfuls, quite regardless of lookers on.

They are so strong as easily to carry me.

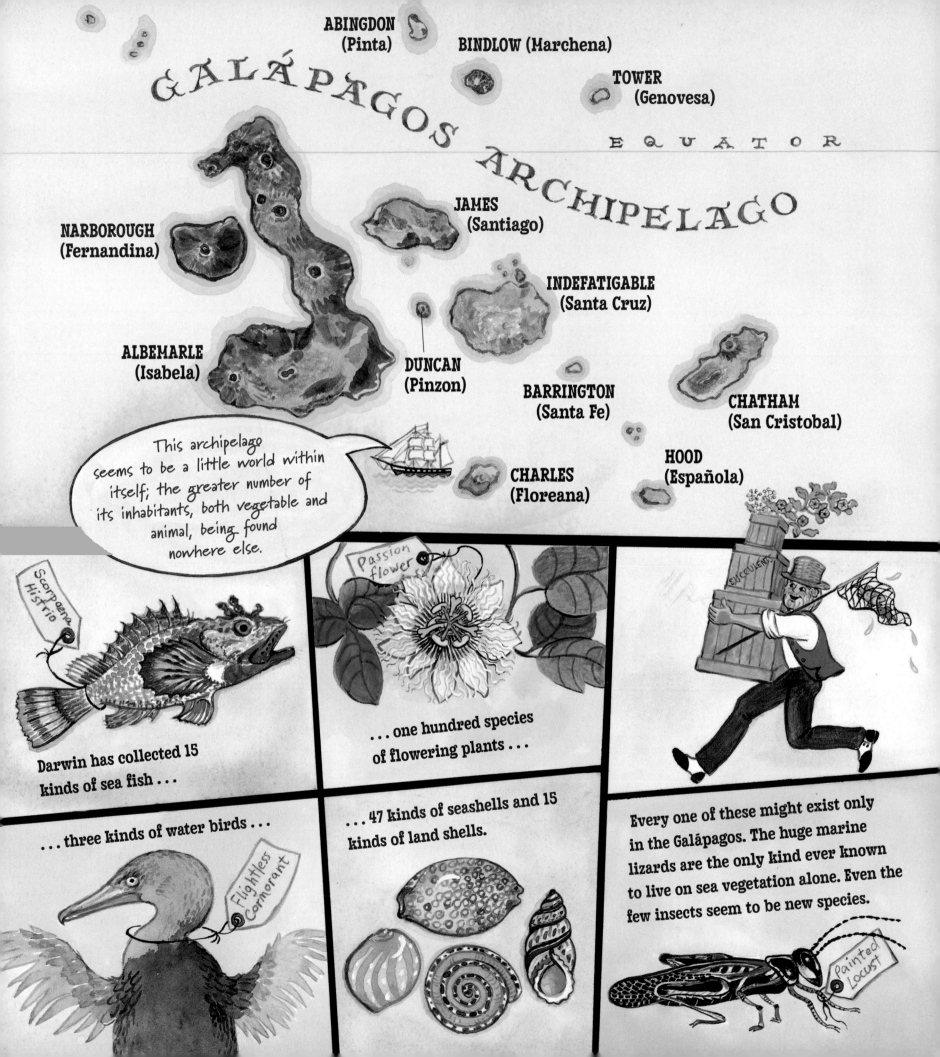

Island Paradise

The *Beagle* heads southwest on a 3,200-mile voyage to Tahiti. At sunrise on November 15, 1835, Darwin spots the steepest and wildest peaks of this fabled isle as they soar above the clouds.

We landed to enjoy all the delights of charming Tahiti. Crowds of men, women & children collected to receive us with laughing merry faces.

These precipices must have been some thousands of feet high; the whole formed a mountain gorge far more magnificent than anything I ever beheld.

Darwin hires two men to guide him straight up a mountain. The Tahitians have come up with all kinds of wonderful ways to live well in their island home.

Shaded by a rock beneath a façade of columnar Lava we ate our dinner. My guide had procured a dish of fish & fresh-water prawns. They carried with them a small net; where the water was deep, they dived & like otters followed the fish into holes & thus secured them. The Tahitians have the dexterity of Amphibious animals in the water.

A little higher a succession of waterfalls descended from the jagged summit. A face of naked rock had to be passed by the aid of ropes. One of the Tahitians, a fine active man, placed the trunk of a tree against this, swarmed up it, & then by the aid of crevices reached the summit. He fixed the ropes to a projecting point & lowered them for us & then hauled up the dog & luggage.

We bivouacked for the night. On each side of a ravine there were great beds of Banana covered with ripe fruit. By the aid of strips of bark for twine, the stems of bamboo, & the large leaf of the banana, the Tahitians in a few minutes built an excellent house & with withered banana leaves made a soft bed.

During the night it rained heavily, but the good thatch of Banana leaves kept us dry.

How to Cook a Meal in Tahiti

1 MAKE A FIRE — Rub — Hibiscus wood

2 Add stones

3 Wild arum tops — Fish — Beef — Ripe and green bananas — Leaf — FOLD UP FOOD PACKETS

4 COOK THE FOOD — Cutaway view of oven (No smoke or steam can escape.) — More earth — Red-hot stones — Food packets — Earth

5 READY TO EAT IN 15 MINUTES — Banana leaf table cloth

6 COOL WATER FROM RUNNING STREAM — Coconut shell cup

7 DINNER IS SERVED — Delicious! — DESSERT — Root of ti plant — Sweet as sugar

33

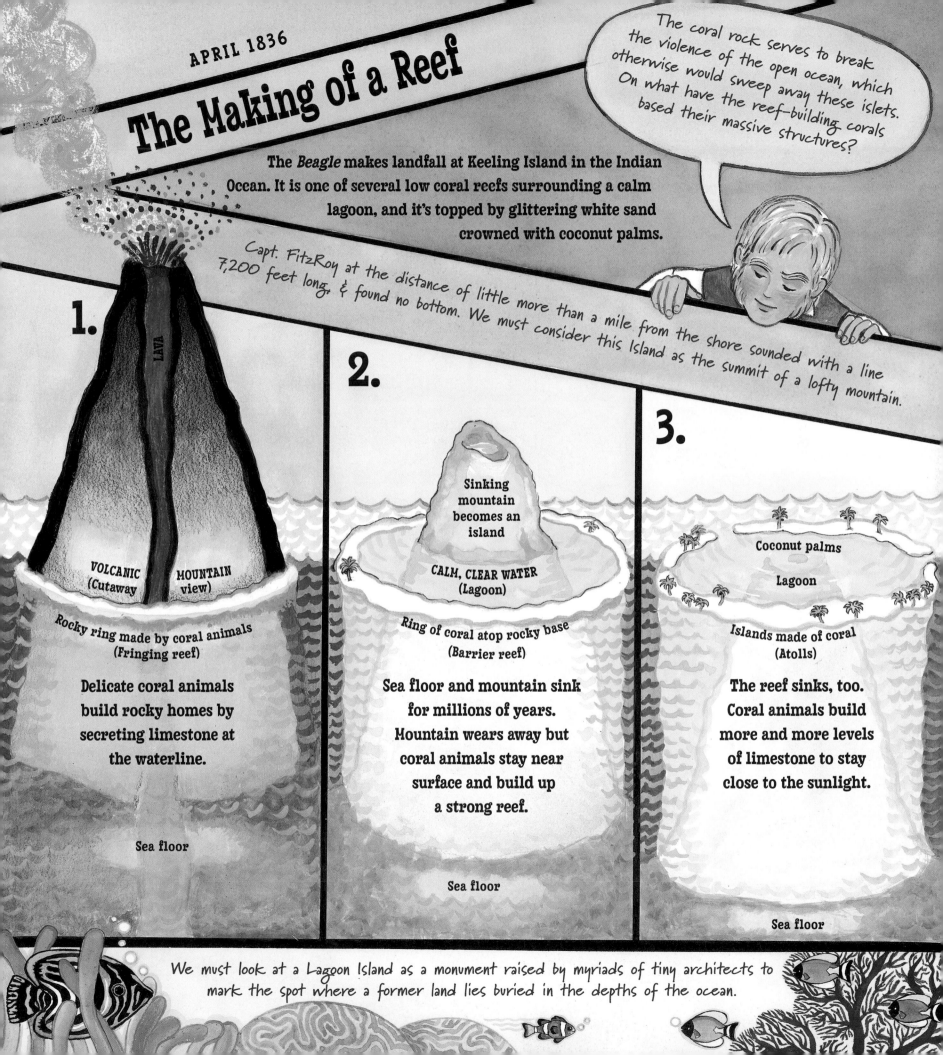

A Few Final Stops

He sees people of many nations mingled together in South Africa . . .

French lady

Malay

Hottentot

Dutchman

The voyagers sail to the isle of Mauritius, where Darwin rides an elephant in true Indian fashion.

. . . writes of red volcanoes and freed slaves in Ascension . . .

. . . and visits the wondrous jungles of Brazil once again when the *Beagle* returns for a final survey.

But by now, everyone aboard is thoroughly homesick.

I loathe, I abhor the sea, & all ships which sail on it.

OCTOBER 1836

Home to England!

After a tolerably short passage but with some very heavy weather, we came to an anchor at Falmouth. I reached home at breakfast time. My head is quite confused with so much delight.

36

And That's Not All

Darwin becomes a secretary of the Geological Society of London . . .

. . . writes a five-volume book about the animals he found . . .

FOSSILS
BIRDS
FISH
REPTILES
MAMMALS

. . . and publishes another book, *The Voyage of the Beagle*, to tell about his travels, discoveries, and adventures.

VOYAGE OF THE BEAGLE

It becomes wildly popular and is sold all around the world.

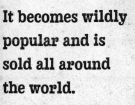

Darwin has always been athletic and full of energy, but when he is only 29 years old, he develops a mysterious ailment that saps his strength and keeps him from leaving England for the rest of his life. In spite of this, however, there is some excellent news.

What Happens Next?

Hardly stopping to take a breath, Darwin gets straight to work. He moves to London for a while, and in less than two years, he classifies over 1,500 species from his enormous *Beagle* collection. He also gets help from four other scientists, who realize that Darwin has found hundreds of plants and animals never before classified by Europeans.

My dear Lyell

I have the very good & unexpected fortune of going to be married. The lady is my cousin Miss Emma Wedgwood. We are connected by manifold ties, besides on my part, by the most sincere love & hearty gratitude to her, for accepting such a one as myself.

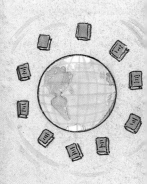

Darwin marries Emma in 1839. They are devoted to each other and will have ten children.

An Astonishing Mystery!

And now Darwin begins his most earthshaking venture of all. Every one of his discoveries during the voyage has opened his eyes to the greatest mystery imaginable. It begs to be solved!

What Is the True History of Life on Earth?

NEW VERSION

OLD VERSION

The official religion of England during Darwin's day is Christianity, so most English people believe the Bible story that says heaven and Earth and all living things were divinely created in six days just a few thousand years ago. Even a majority of scientists think that each plant and animal—including man himself—looked exactly the same at the moment of creation as it does right now. Darwin himself grew up with a firm belief in this idea.

Darwin's own grandfather and a few other thinkers had long proposed that over millions of years all living things must have descended from a mere handful of ancestors. Yet not one person had ever proven how or why such evolution took place. Until now.

> I did not then in the least doubt the literal truth of every word in the Bible. Disbelief crept over me at a very slow rate, but was at last complete.

Darwin now believes that living things have never stayed the same and that they will continue to evolve forever. Very secretly, he sets out to prove it.

The Tree of Life
Darwin's Theory of Evolution

Millions or billions of years ago, the first spark of life took root in a tiny number of extremely primitive beings—or maybe only a single one—from which every kind of living thing on Earth has now descended. Darwin compares the creation of new beings to an ancient tree that constantly sprouts new branches.

From so simple a beginning endless forms most beautiful and most wonderful have been, and are being, evolved.

Clues & Hard Questions

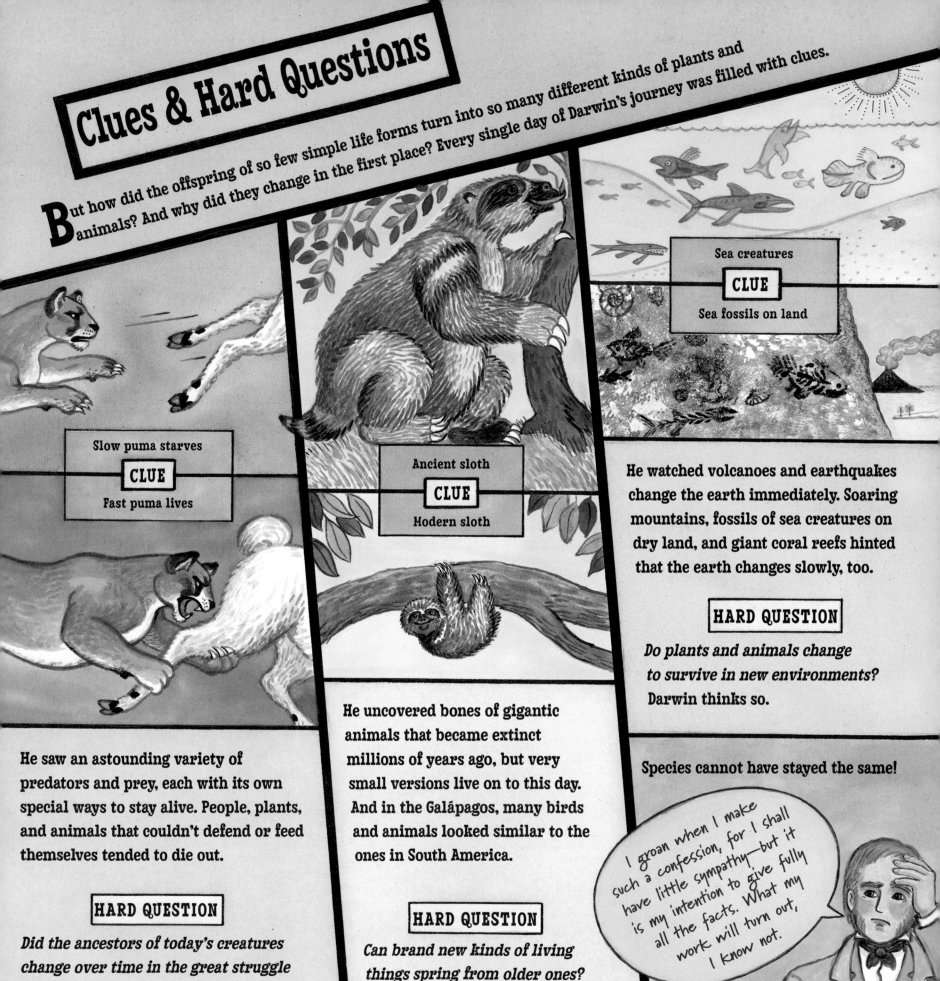

Slow puma starves

CLUE

Fast puma lives

Ancient sloth

CLUE

Modern sloth

Sea creatures

CLUE

Sea fossils on land

He watched volcanoes and earthquakes change the earth immediately. Soaring mountains, fossils of sea creatures on dry land, and giant coral reefs hinted that the earth changes slowly, too.

HARD QUESTION

Do plants and animals change to survive in new environments? Darwin thinks so.

Species cannot have stayed the same!

He saw an astounding variety of predators and prey, each with its own special ways to stay alive. People, plants, and animals that couldn't defend or feed themselves tended to die out.

He uncovered bones of gigantic animals that became extinct millions of years ago, but very small versions live on to this day. And in the Galápagos, many birds and animals looked similar to the ones in South America.

HARD QUESTION

Did the ancestors of today's creatures change over time in the great struggle to survive?

HARD QUESTION

Can brand new kinds of living things spring from older ones?

I groan when I make such a confession, for I shall have little sympathy—but it is my intention to give fully all the facts. What my work will turn out, I know not.

40

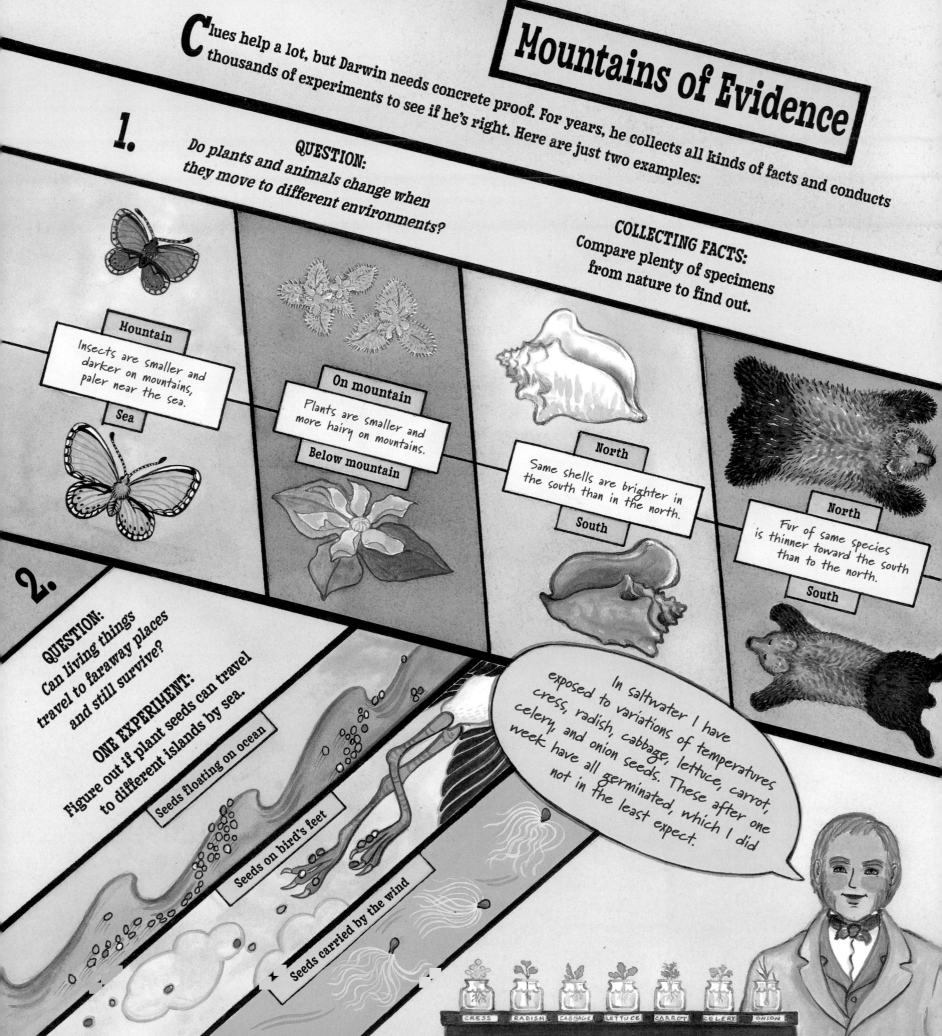

How Evolution Works

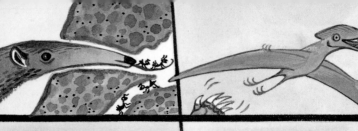

Finally Darwin gathers enough evidence to back up his theory.

Each individual in every species varies slightly in size, color, weight, and so on.

So over a very long time, all species naturally change bit by bit. If some new trait makes life better and survival easier, it will keep passing down from one generation to the next.

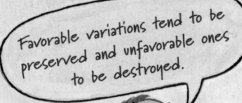

Favorable variations tend to be preserved and unfavorable ones to be destroyed.

After many generations of tiny helpful changes, old species eventually turn into brand new ones. What kind of changes might help?

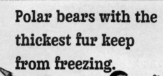

Anteaters with the longest snouts reach the most ants.

Animals evolve wings to escape predators . . . or to catch prey.

Polar bears with the thickest fur keep from freezing.

Compound eyes let flies detect enemy movements faster.

Upright posture and the ability to talk leads to civilization.

All animals try their hardest to attract the best mates. (That's what some colorful butterfly wings and curling horns are for.) And good mates pass good traits to the next generations.

Birds of paradise congregate, and successive males show off their gorgeous plumage; they likewise perform strange antics before the females, which at last choose the most attractive partner.

Male alligators fight, bellow, and whirl round like Indians in a war-dance for the possession of the females; male stag beetles bear wounds from the huge mandibles of other males.

Over millions of years, living things have multiplied enormously and have spread around the world. Plants and animals now live everywhere, so different kinds of species must evolve to survive in all kinds of places.

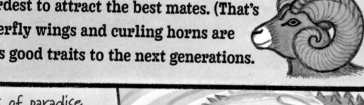

Lots of animals that look completely different have evolved from the same ancestor!
What clues helped Darwin find out? Take bones for example:

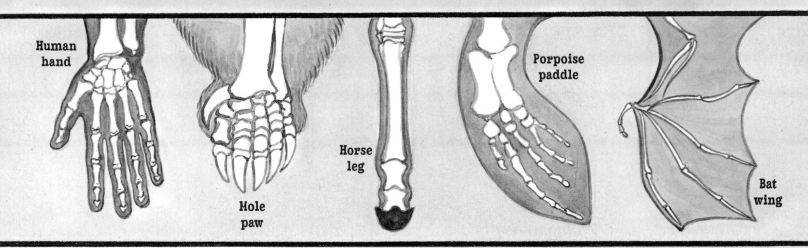

Human hand

Mole paw

Horse leg

Porpoise paddle

Bat wing

What can be more curious than that the hand of a man, formed for grasping, that of a mole for digging, the leg of the horse, the paddle of the porpoise, and the wing of the bat, should all be constructed on the same pattern, and should include the same bones, in the same relative positions?

Living things that can't find food, catch prey, attract good mates, or escape from predators, diseases, natural disasters, and harsh climates will die out. This may sound terrible, but it's not.

Every organic being naturally increases at so high a rate that if [most are] not destroyed, the earth would soon be covered by [the offspring of] a single pair.

The elephant is the slowest breeder of all known animals. Assume that it breeds when thirty years old and goes on breeding till ninety years old, bringing forth three pair of young; at the end of the fifth century, there would be fifteen million elephants descended from the first pair.

Just think what would happen if all the thousands of seeds from a single weed survived and each new weed produced thousands more seeds that all survived. Their offspring would soon cover the earth and choke out everything else. That's why every plant and animal must struggle to live, and only the fittest (or the luckiest) can survive. The rest become extinct.

I have called this principle, by which each slight variation, if useful, is preserved, by the term Natural Selection. I am convinced that Natural Selection has been the most important, but not the exclusive, means of modification.

Almost Scooped

In spite of all his hard work, Darwin doesn't publish his findings for 20 years! Why not?

I had at last got a theory by which to work; but I was so anxious to avoid prejudice, that I determined not to write even the briefest sketch of it.

Worried that his ideas will create a ruckus over the Bible's version of creation, he keeps the results of his studies a secret, sharing only bits and pieces with a few fellow scientists he trusts and respects.

The world might never have found out about Darwin's secret theory. But in June 1858, Darwin receives a bulky essay from the Malay Archipelago halfway around the world.

ALFRED RUSSEL WALLACE

Unknowingly, a scientist named Alfred Russel Wallace has come up with a theory that is basically the same as Darwin's, although unlike Darwin, he hasn't done the scientific studies to prove it. He asks Darwin to forward the essay to the famous scientist Charles Lyell, who is Darwin's good friend. With a sinking heart, Darwin writes this letter:

SIR CHARLES LYELL

My dear Lyell

Wallace has to-day sent me the enclosed & asked me to forward it to you. It seems to me well worth reading. Your words have come true with a vengeance that I should be forestalled. If Wallace had my manuscript sketch written out in 1842 he could not have made a better short abstract! Even his terms now stand as Heads of my Chapters.

I shall of course at once write & offer to send [his work] to any Journal. So all my originality, whatever it may amount to, will be smashed. I hope you will approve of Wallace's sketch, that I may tell him what you say.

Yours most truly,

C. Darwin

The Secret Unveiled!

Lyell and another scientist already know about Darwin's years of study. They urge him not to hide his findings any longer. Darwin's work is presented along with Wallace's at a scientific meeting on July 1, and a year later, Darwin finally releases his book *On the Origin of Species*. The first edition sells out in a single day.

I am infinitely pleased and proud at the appearance of my child.

Darwin is right to think his work will cause an uproar. Some call him brilliant; others are furious to think that man could be descended from animals.

On June 30, 1860, a scientific meeting in Oxford overflows with spectators fascinated by evolution. Darwin is sick and can't come. The first speaker is as dull as dishwater.

But when powerful Bishop Samuel Wilberforce loudly begins to condemn Darwin's book, a rowdy argument breaks out.

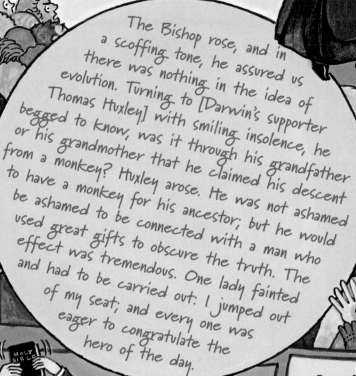

The Bishop rose, and in a scoffing tone, he assured us there was nothing in the idea of evolution. Turning to [Darwin's supporter Thomas Huxley] with smiling insolence, he begged to know, was it through his grandfather or his grandmother that he claimed his descent from a monkey? Huxley arose. He was not ashamed to have a monkey for his ancestor; but he would be ashamed to be connected with a man who used great gifts to obscure the truth. The effect was tremendous. One lady fainted and had to be carried out. I jumped out of my seat; and every one was eager to congratulate the hero of the day.

Just then, a gentleman raises a Bible over his head, begging the audience to follow the word of God rather than man. He is none other than Robert FitzRoy, the former captain of the *Beagle*, and he's horrified by his old friend's book! The crowd shouts him down.

Darwin is glad he wasn't there. Even so, in a letter to Huxley, he says:

From all I hear, it seems that Oxford did the subject great good. It is of enormous importance, showing the world that a few first-rate men are not afraid of expressing their opinion.

Evolution on the March

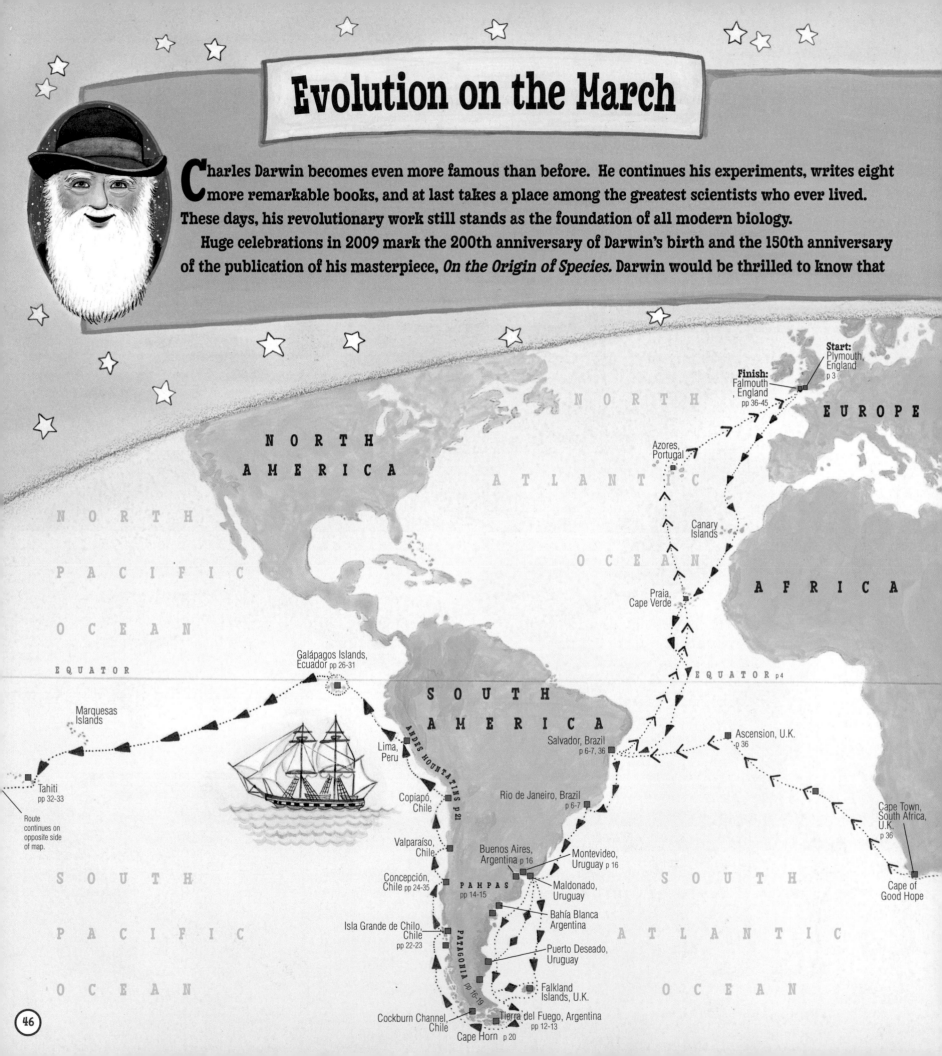

Charles Darwin becomes even more famous than before. He continues his experiments, writes eight more remarkable books, and at last takes a place among the greatest scientists who ever lived. These days, his revolutionary work still stands as the foundation of all modern biology.

Huge celebrations in 2009 mark the 200th anniversary of Darwin's birth and the 150th anniversary of the publication of his masterpiece, *On the Origin of Species*. Darwin would be thrilled to know that

NORTH AMERICA

NORTH PACIFIC OCEAN

NORTH ATLANTIC OCEAN

EUROPE

AFRICA

Start: Plymouth, England p 3

Finish: Falmouth, England pp 36-45

Azores, Portugal

Canary Islands

Praia, Cape Verde

EQUATOR

EQUATOR p 4

SOUTH AMERICA

Galápagos Islands, Ecuador pp 26-31

Marquesas Islands

Lima, Peru

Ascension, U.K. p 36

Salvador, Brazil p 6-7, 36

Tahiti pp 32-33

Route continues on opposite side of map.

ANDES MOUNTAINS p 21

Copiapó, Chile

Rio de Janeiro, Brazil p 6-7

Valparaíso, Chile

Buenos Aires, Argentina p 16

Montevideo, Uruguay p 16

Cape Town, South Africa, U.K. p 36

Concepción, Chile pp 24-35

PAHPAS

Maldonado, Uruguay

Cape of Good Hope

Bahía Blanca Argentina

Isla Grande de Chilo, Chile pp 22-23

PATAGONIA pp 16-19

Puerto Deseado, Uruguay

SOUTH PACIFIC OCEAN

SOUTH ATLANTIC OCEAN

Falkland Islands, U.K.

Cockburn Channel, Chile

Tierra del Fuego, Argentina pp 12-13

Cape Horn p 20

overwhelming scientific evidence firmly establishes evolution as a proven fact and new scientific techniques have filled in many of the blanks in the history of life on Earth.

Yet even as we read this page celebrating Darwin's life and work, our planet is changing every minute. As the number of people grows by leaps and bounds, multitudes of wild animals, fish, and birds are becoming endangered or extinct. Rain forests, wetlands, farmland, valuable natural resources, and even the air we breathe are gravely threatened. Will future scientists find ways to help us survive? Or will human beings and all the other living things of today vanish forever as brand-new creatures evolve to take our places?

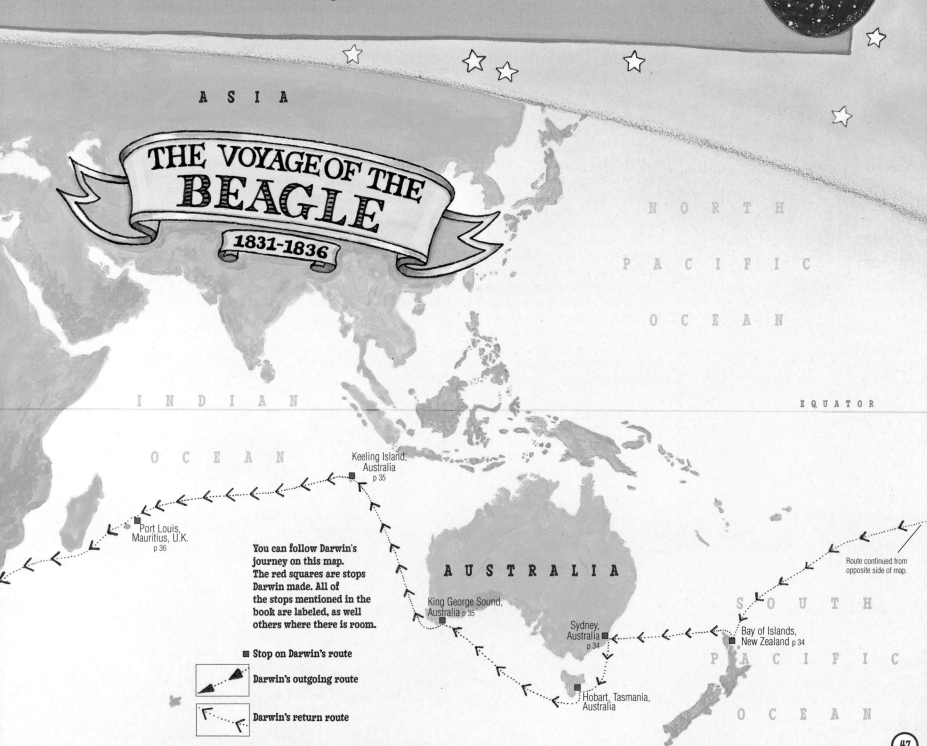

ASIA

THE VOYAGE OF THE BEAGLE

1831–1836

NORTH PACIFIC OCEAN

INDIAN OCEAN

EQUATOR

Keeling Island, Australia p 35

Port Louis, Mauritius, U.K. p 36

You can follow Darwin's journey on this map. The red squares are stops Darwin made. All of the stops mentioned in the book are labeled, as well others where there is room.

Route continued from opposite side of map.

AUSTRALIA

King George Sound, Australia p 35

Sydney, Australia p 34

Bay of Islands, New Zealand p 34

SOUTH PACIFIC OCEAN

■ Stop on Darwin's route

Darwin's outgoing route

Darwin's return route

Hobart, Tasmania, Australia

Index

Author's Note

I loved everything about making this book. Inspired by the small role my grandfather played in the Scopes Monkey Trial (see the dedication), I set out do more than learn about the adventurous young Charles Darwin. I wanted as much as possible to get inside his head so that I could share his vision with young people.

First came a voyage of my own. The gigantic iguanas I saw in the Galapagos looked like volcanic rocks with attitude, and I could stand right next to each fearless bird and lumbering tortoise. These. along with Ecuador's iridescent hummingbirds and butterflies and forests dripping with orchids, filled up my camera with over 3,000 pictures.

Then came reading, reading, and more reading. Charles Darwin was a natural storyteller. As he traveled around the world, he kept a diary filled with good humor, tales of adventure, and a sense of wonder and enthusiasm about each new discovery he made. Reading his diary confirmed my hopes that I could tell Darwin's story largely in his own words. I also read several of his other works as well as his letters (see the bibliography) and many secondary sources to round out my understanding of the journey of the Beagle and what happened after that.

For the illustrations, I chose acrylics and a graphic novel layout with lots of diagonals to communicate Darwin's rich (almost overwhelming) sensory and intellectual experience on the voyage as well as the motion of the journey. It was also fun to make him age just a bit on every page.

As in my previous books, I focused on making the drawings accurate. In addition to relying on my own photographs, I based many illustrations on drawings and paintings by artists who sailed with Darwin or followed his route later. I also scoured museum photos of fossils, satellite photos, and my own extensive picture collection of places around the world, animals, clothing, architecture, and more.

For Darwin's follow-up research and how he came to his conclusions, I am indebted to Darwin himself and to the secondary sources listed here. I especially enjoyed reading James D. Watson, Jonathan Weiner, and Edward O. Wilson, and perusing the American Museum of Natural History Web site curated by Niles Eldredge.

Sources

All of the quotes used in this book are from the sources listed below. There isn't room to list exact locations for each quote here, but you can access that information by visiting www.rosalynschanzer.com/DarwinSources.html.QuoteSources.htmi

Bibliography

Barlow, Nora, ed. *Charles Darwin's Diary of the Voyage of H.M.S. Beagle.* Cambridge: Cambridge University Press, 1933.

Burkhardt, Frederick, ed. *Charles Darwin's Letters; A Selection 1825-1859.* New York: Cambridge University Press, 1996.

Darwin, Charles, Francis Darwin, Albert Charles Seward. *More Letters of Charles Darwin: A Record of His Work in a Series of Hitherto Unpublished Letters.* New York: D. Appleton and Company, 1903.

Darwin, Charles. *Journal of Researches into the Natural History and Geology of the Countries Visited During the Voyage of H.M.S. Beagle Round the World, Under the Command of Capt. Fitz Roy, R.N.* 2d edition. London: John Murray, 1845.

Darwin, Charles. *Narrative of the Surveying Voyages of His Majesty's Ships Adventure and Beagle Between the Years 1826 and 1836, Describing Their Examination of the Southern Shores of South America, and the Beagle's Circumnavigation of the Globe.* Journal and Remarks. 1832-1836. London: Henry Colburn, 1839.

Darwin, Charles. "Notes on *Rhea americana* and *Rhea darwinii*." *Proceedings of the Zoological Society of London* 5 (1837): 35–36, 1837.

Darwin, Charles. *On the Origin of Species by Means of Natural Selection, or the Preservation of Favoured Races in the Struggle for Life.* London: John Murray, 1859.

Darwin, Francis, ed. *Charles Darwin: His Life Told in an Autobiographical Chapter, and in a Selected Series of His Unpublished Letters.* London: John Murray, 1892.

Darwin, Francis, ed. *The Life and Letters of Charles Darwin, Including an Autobiographical Chapter,* vol. 1. London: John Murray, 1887.

Darwin, Francis. "FitzRoy and Darwin, 1831–36." *Nature: A Weekly Illustrated Journal of Science* 88 (12 February, 1912): 547–8.

Desmond, Adrian, and James Moore. *Darwin: The Life of a Tormented Evolutionist.* New York: Warner Books, 1991.

Eldredge, Niles, curator. "Darwin." American Museum of Natural History, 2005. http://www.amnh.org/exhibitions/darwin/

Eldredge, Niles. *Darwin: Discovering the Tree of Life.* New York: W. W. Norton & Company, 2005.

"Evolution and Natural Selection" (lecture). University of Michigan Global Change Curriculum. http://www.globalchange.umich.edu/globalchange1/current/lectures/selection/selection.html 2005

Huxley, Thomas, and Leonard Huxley. *Life and Letters of Thomas Henry Huxley,* Volume 1. New York: D. Appleton and Company, 1916.

Keynes, Richard, ed. *Charles Darwin's Beagle Diary.* Cambridge: Cambridge University Press, 2001.

Moorehead, Alan. *Darwin and the Beagle.* New York: Penguin, 1971.

Nichols, Peter. *Evolution's Captain: The Story of the Kidnapping that Led to Charles Darwin's Voyage Aboard the "Beagle."* New York: Perennial, 2004.

Quammen, David. *The Reluctant Mr. Darwin: An Intimate Portrait of Charles Darwin and the Making of His Theory of Evolution.* New York: Atlas Books and W. W. Norton & Company, 2006.

van Wyhe, John, curator. The Complete Works of Charles Darwin Online. http://darwin-online.org.uk.

Watson, James D., ed. *Darwin: The Indelible Stamp.* Philadelphia: Running Press, 2005.

Weiner, Jonathan. *The Beak of the Finch.* New York: Vintage Books, 1995.

Wilson, Edward O., ed. *From So Simple a Beginning: The Four Great Books of Charles Darwin.* New York: W. W. Norton & Company, 2006.